異文化理解おもしろクイズ

永倉 由里

開拓社

ま え が き

　「異文化理解を促す英語教育の実践」を心がけ，あれこれ工夫を重ねるようになってから10年近くが過ぎた。当初は，'外国語学習には該当言語の背景にある「文化」の理解は欠かせない' という程度の簡単な理由付けをしていた。

　しかし，実践と並行してその意義を整理してみると，言語の習得だけにとどまらぬ大きな効果があることに気づき，驚きさえも感じている。

　そもそも，私たちの一生が，自分とは異なる文化をもつ様々な人たちとの直接的あるいは間接的な関わり合いで成り立っていることに着目すれば，生きることは「異文化とのコミュニケーション」の連続だと捉えることができる。となれば，異文化理解を促すことに力点を置いた教育実践が，みなさん方，若い方々の人間形成にもかなりの影響があるのではないだろうか。

　これまでの実践から言うと，異文化に対する理解が進み，そのことを認識し始めると，顔つきが変わってくる。知識・情報を柔軟に受け入れ，ぐんぐん吸収するようになる。そして，問題意識が高まり，自分の意見を持つようになるので，意見交換が可能になる。こうしたみなさんの知的好奇心の高まりは，私たち教師を刺激することにもなる。まさに '良いこと尽くめ' である。

　さて，学習において大切なのは，やはり"授業"。テーマに関心が持て，積極的に活動し，しかもきちんと定着させることができれば申し分ない。そこで，異文化への気づきを促す教材を作り，楽しい活動を引き出したいと考えた。

　本書は，主に生活文化・言語文化の相違に気づかせるワン・ポイント・クイズ形式のもの，コミュニケーションの際に起こりうる誤解や勘違いを盛り込んだダイアローグ形式のもの，さらに，人権問題など，現代社会が抱える諸問題につながるものなどで構成されている。

　この『異文化理解おもしろクイズ』を通して，一人でも多くのみなさんが「へぇ～，なるほど！」「ふ～ん，そうなの？」と面白みを感じ，積極的に外国語を学んでほしい。本書が，人と人との関わりの基盤である「実践的コミュニケーション能力」を養うためのトレーニングに活用されることを祈ってやまない。

　　平成16年3月30日

　　　　　　　　　　　　　　　　　　　　　　　　　　　　永 倉 由 里

目　次	概　　要	頁
1．外国人が感じる日本の「ふしぎ」		
1　Good Taste!?	「汗」を飲むの？	5
2　Logotype	Tシャツにギョッとするようなロゴが…	6
3　Mask	日本はお医者さんだらけ？	6
4　ZZZ ZZZ ZZZ …	どうしてどこでも眠れるの？	7
5　Domo	「どうも」ばっかりで？？？	7
2．英語で遊ぼう！　Fun Time		
6　Bowwow（カルタ付き）	動物の鳴き声や擬声音の日米比較。	9
7　Tongue-twister	英語の早口ことばに挑戦！	11
8　Hot Dog	語源を探ろう！	12
9　?	語源を探ろう！	12
10　Tennis	語源を探ろう！	13
11　Wedding	語源を探ろう！	13
12　Sneeze	くしゃみをしたら…	14
13　XYZ	XYZって何のこと？	14
14　Jokes	英米人のジョークを味わってみよう。	15
3．アメリカ人の知らない英語		
15　アメリカ人の知らない英語(1)	morning service（英：日曜の礼拝）	16
16　アメリカ人の知らない英語(2)	トレパン（日）／training pants（英：赤ちゃん用パンツ）	17
17　アメリカ人の知らない英語(3)	ヒアリングテスト（日）／hearing test（英：聴力検査）	18
18　アメリカ人の知らない英語(4)	マフラー（日）／muffler（英：車の部品）	19
19　アメリカ人の知らない英語(5)	Japanese English に要注意！	20
20　ガイジンを悩ませる英語(1)	日本人が間違えやすい表現。	21
21　ガイジンを悩ませる英語(2)	日本人が間違えやすい表現。	22
4．知っておきたい英語の知識		
22　Metaphor	Back-seat-driver ってどんな人？	23
23　Body	からだの部位を使った表現。	24
24　Colors	色に対するイメージも異なるようです。	24
25　アメリカ英語とイギリス英語(1)	デパートで待ち合わせ。ところが…	26
26　アメリカ英語とイギリス英語(2)	単語，発音，つづりの違いをチェック！	27
27　L & R (1)	発音に注意しよう！	28
28　L & R (2)	正しく発音しないと，とんでもない意味に…	29
29　Misleading Pronunciation	聞き分けにくい語句を集めてみました。	30
30　will と be going to	全く同じ意味だと思っていませんか？	31
5．英語の「構え」でコミュニケーション		
31　Gestures (1)	まずはダイアローグで。	32
32　Gestures (2)	今度はイラストで。	33
33　同意の合いの手	会話の潤滑油，合いの手を身につけよう。	34
34　うながす合いの手	会話の潤滑油，合いの手を身につけよう。	35
35　驚きの合いの手	会話の潤滑油，合いの手を身につけよう。	36
36　Come On	状況や言い方によって様々な意味に。	37
37　How Can I Answer It?	日本に暮らす外国人が尋ねられて困る質問。	38

38	Small Talk (1)	会話の潤滑油, Small Talk を身につけよう。	39
39	Small Talk (2)	会話の潤滑油, Small Talk を身につけよう。	40

6. 生活文化から生じるコミュニケーション・ギャップ

40	Souvenirs	贈り物をもらったら,すぐあける(英米)／あけない(日)	41
41	Toilet	未使用のトイレのドア：開(英米)／閉(日)	42
42	Guest	客に家の中を案内する(英米)／しない(日)	43
43	Tea Time	意思表示があいまい(日)	44
44	In the Classroom	教師の問いかけに対し沈黙する生徒(日)	45
45	In the Teachers' Room	ほめ言葉：頻繁でオーバー(英米)	46
46	Hiccups	しゃっくりの止め方(英米)／(日)	47
47	Nodding	うなづき：同意を示す(英米)／聞いているだけ(日)	48
48	The Japanese Smile	照れ笑い(日)	49
49	Either Will Do	あいまいな返事(日)	50
50	Etiquette	おそばをすする音(日)／ハンカチで鼻をかむ(英米)	51
51	Invitation	社交辞令的な招待(日)	52
52	Family	身内をほめる(英米)／けなす(日)	53

7. 知っておきたい一般知識

53	Halloween	おなじみの年中行事の意味をご存じですか。	54
54	Christmas	クリスマス, サンタ・クロースについてのクイズ。	55
55	Traffic Signs	交通標識の日米比較。	56
56	Emergency	110番は世界共通？	57
57	Oh My God!	なぜか「捨て台詞」に神様が…	58
58	Who Are These People?	これくらいは知っておきたい偉人8人。	59
59	Witty Remarks	有名人が残したためになる一言。	60
60	Quiz about the USA	アメリカ合衆国についての一般的質問。	61
61	Quiz about the UK	英国についての一般的質問。	62
62	A Rolling Stone	所変われば, 諺の意味も…	63
63	Proverbs	諺：集団主義(日)と個人主義(英米)が見えてくる。	64

8. 異文化間に生じる諸問題を考えよう！

64	ALTs from the USA	全員アメリカ出身のALTですが…	65
65	Vegetable Soup	多民族国家アメリカの意識の変化。	66
66	PC (= Politically Correct)	政治的に正しい表現(米)	67
67	Stereotypes	他文化に対する偏見をチェックしてみよう。	68
68	Who Are the Japanese?	国際結婚に海外勤務。日本人とはどんな人？	69
69	Roots	名字を見ればルーツがわかる。	70
70	アメリカ映画の中のニッポン	アメリカ映画の中に描かれた日本人像（ビデオ）。	71
71	映画で学ぶ人権と差別(1)	映画で差別問題にアプローチ。	73
72	映画で学ぶ人権と差別(2)	例として感動の名作をあげました。	74
73	映画で学ぶ人権と差別(3)	実際に映画を見て感想をまとめてみよう。	75
74	青い目茶色い目	エリオット先生の反人種差別教育。	76
75	Martin Luther King Quiz	キング牧師についての質問。	77
付録	カルタ3種	Bowwow, アメリカ人の知らない英語, ことわざ。	78

1. 外国人が感じる日本の「ふしぎ」

異文化理解の第一歩は自らの文化を理解すること。日本に接した外国人の方々は，どんなことに戸惑い，どんなことに驚いているのでしょうか。

異文化理解 おもしろクイズ 1	Good Taste!?

Q. Why are many foreigners surprised in these cases? Choose suitable words from the list below.

1. *Gaijins* find it difficult to swallow some drinks named (　　).
2. *Gaijins* find it difficult to swallow some drinks which sounds like (　　).
3. *Gaijins* don't like to drink coffee with some powder whose name reminds them how the insects (　　).

> ア．jump　　イ．sweat　　ウ．cow piss　　エ．creep

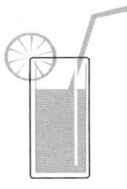

| 異文化理解 おもしろクイズ | 2 | Logotype |

Q. Look at the photos and imagine the foreigner's feelings.

 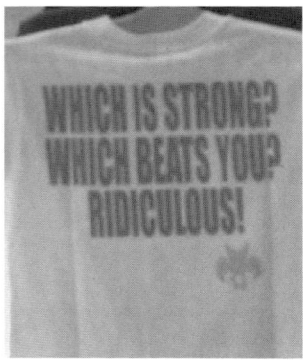 

Don't you know the meaning of these logotypes?

| 異文化理解 おもしろクイズ | 3 | Mask |

Q. Look at the cartoon and imagine the foreigner's feelings.

| 異文化理解 おもしろクイズ | 4 | ZZZ ZZZ ZZZ ... |

Q. Look at the cartoons and imagine the foreigner's feelings.

A1. How can Japanese people sleep on the trains? Unbelievable!
A2. Japanese people must be very tired. I'm sorry for them.
A3. Japanese people are very rude. Incredible!

| 異文化理解 おもしろクイズ | 5 | Domo |

Q1. Look at the cartoons and put the expressions into English.

1.「いやぁ，どうも」

2.「どうも(お疲れ様)」

3.「どうも(ありがとう)」

4.「どうも(すみません)」

5.「どうも（はじめまして）」   7.「このたびはどうも（ご愁傷様）」

6.「納豆はどうも…」

Q2. Read the story and choose suitable words from the list below. The following was written by an American businessman.

Japanese people use "domo" very often. At first I thought it meant "(1)." When a woman dropped a handkerchief and I picked it up for her, she said, "Domo."

A few days later, I found another meaning. A woman stood waiting for someone. She looked angry. At last her friend came running. Then he said, "Domo domo."

So I understood this word as "thank you" or "(2)." Perhaps "arigatou" or "sumimasen" comes after "domo."

Why don't they say it in full? Is the Japanese way to say things? How do they know what their partners are going to say?

Only recently I learned some more meanings. When two people meet, they say, "Iya domo." And then when they part, again they say, "Ja domo." Does "domo" mean "(3)," or "(4)"?

"Domo domo" is very complicated for me.

```
ア． see you
イ． I'm sorry
ウ． thank you
エ． hello
```

Domo Domo   *Domo Domo*
Domo Domo

2. 英語で遊ぼう！ Fun Time

動物の鳴き声・人が出す音・物音は、日本語とはずいぶん違う。カルタ遊びの要領で、ペア・ワークやクラス・ワークをしてみよう。泣き声入りスキット、物音入りスキットにも挑戦しよう！　早口言葉や「へぇ〜」と驚く語源や英米人ならではのジョークも紹介する。

異文化理解 おもしろクイズ	6	Bowwow

Look at the pictures and choose suitable words from below.

- ア．squeak
- イ．cock-a-doodle-doo
- ウ．quack-quack
- エ．moo
- オ．croak croak
- カ．bowwow
- キ．meow
- ク．oink-oink
- ケ．chirp-chirp
- コ．caw-caw
- サ．baa baa
- シ．neigh

ス. ouch　　　セ. glug glug　　　ソ. bla bla　　　タ. cough cough
チ. gobble　　ツ. yahoo　　　　 テ. brrr　　　　 ト. wow
ナ. achoo　　 ニ. boo hoo　　　 ヌ. kitchy-kitchy　ネ. zzz
ノ. munch munch　ハ. oops　　　ヒ. clap clap　　 フ. eek

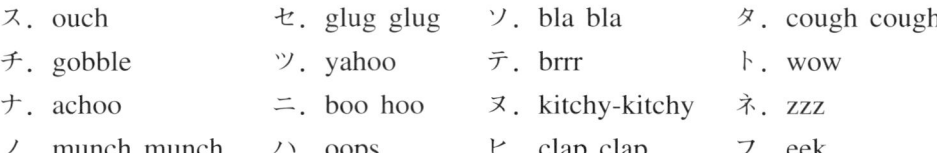

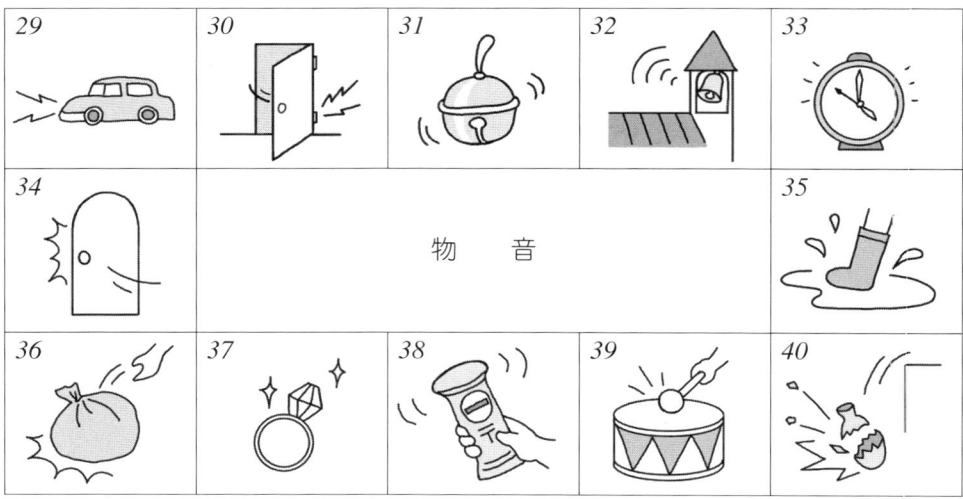

ヘ. smash　　　ホ. tick-tock　　　　マ. ding-dong　　　　ミ. bang
ム. twinkle　　 メ. ting-a-ling-a-ling　モ. splash　　　　　ヤ. beep
ユ. thud　　　　ヨ. creak　　　　　 ラ. rum-pa-pum-pum　リ. jingle-jingle

異文化理解 おもしろクイズ 7　Tongue-twister

Try to say the following sentences quickly and clearly.

(1)　A big black bug bit a big black bear.

(2)　The sun shines on shop signs.

(3)　I bought a box of biscuits and a box of mixed biscuits.

(4)　Each Easter Eddie eats eighty Easter Eggs.

(5)　She sells sea-shells on the seashore,
　　　The shells she sells are sea-shells, I'm sure,
　　　For if she sells sea-shells on the seashore,
　　　Then I'm sure she sells seashore shells.

(6)　Peter Piper picked a peck of pickled peppers;
　　　A peck of pickled peppers Peter Piper picked.
　　　If Peter Piper picked a peck of pickled peppers,
　　　Where's the peck of pickled peppers Peter Piper picked?

(7)　Swan swam over the sea.
　　　Swim, swan, swim!
　　　Swan swam back again!
　　　Well swum, swan!

(8)　Supercalifragilisticexpialidocious

Q.　Which is the most difficult/the easiest for you to say?

	(1)	(2)	(3)	(4)	(5)	(6)	(7)	(8)
3回ずつ読んで自己評価 A（うまい!）B（まあまあ）C（だ～め）								
パートナーに評価してもらおう A（うまい!）B（まあまあ）C（だ～め）								

異文化理解 おもしろクイズ 8 — Hot Dog

Q. Do you like this food?
What do you call it?
Why do people call this delicious food by the name of an animal?

異文化理解 おもしろクイズ 9 — ?

Q. What do you call **?** ?   Why does **?** mean a question?

How about **@** and **&** ?

| 異文化理解 おもしろクイズ | 10 | Tennis |

Q. What is the score, zero, called in tennis matches? And why?

| 異文化理解 おもしろクイズ | 11 | Wedding |

Q. Why does the bride stand to the right of the bridegroom?

| 異文化理解 おもしろクイズ | 12 | Sneeze |

Q. What do English-speaking people say when someone sneezes? And why?

| 異文化理解 おもしろクイズ | 13 | XYZ |

Mr. Yoshida has just moved to Chicago on business. Someone from behind said in a small voice, "XYZ."

Q. What does it mean?

異文化理解 おもしろクイズ 14　Jokes

Q. Try to answer the questions by using lateral thinking.

1. Q: A man rode into town on Sunday. Two days later he rode home on Sunday. How is this possible?
   A: His horse's _____ is _____.

2. Q: A father and his son were in a car accident. The father died. The son was taken to the hospital. The doctor came in and said: I can't do surgery on him, because he's my son. Who was the doctor?
   A: The doctor was his _____.

3. Q: What's got a head and a tail but no body?
   A: A _____.

4. Q: What's got waves but no sea?
   A: My _____.

5. I was arrested at the airport, just because I was greeting my cousin Jack! All that I said was "_____," but very loud.

6. Q: What did the zero say to the eight?
   A: Nice _____.

7. Q: Which room has no doors or windows?
   A: A _____.

8. A: Hey, man! Please call me a taxi.
   B: Yes, sir. You are a _____.

9. Q: What can't be used until it's broken?
   A: An _____.

10. Q: Why is the A like a flower?
    A: Because the _____ is after it.

— 15

3. アメリカ人の知らない英語

日本語には, 非常にたくさんの「カタカナ英語」「Japanese English」が含まれている。てっきり通じると思ってそのまま使うと, まったく通じず怪訝な顔をされたり, 失礼になったりすることもある。要注意！

異文化理解 おもしろクイズ 15　アメリカ人の知らない英語(1)

Read the following dialogue and answer the question below.

Hiroko is a Japanese student, who has just come to Seattle and started a new life as a student at Seattle Community College. She enters a coffee shop for the first time.

(Around 10:00 in the morning)

Waitress:　Can I help you?

Hiroko:　　Well, can I have a morning service, please?

Waitress:　....... (??????) Would you say that again?

Hiroko:　　A morning service, please?

Waitress:　I'm sorry, but we don't have that.

Hiroko:　　(I just want to have a light breakfast here. I wonder why they have no morning service.)

Q.　What does the waitress think?

A1.　Her pronunciation is terrible, I can't understand her.

A2.　She is so rude.

A3.　In fact we don't have what she ordered.

A4.　Should I tell her where the nearest church is?

| 異文化理解 おもしろクイズ | 16 アメリカ人の知らない英語(2) |

Read the following dialogue and answer the question below.

Hiroko is shopping with her roommate, Laura.

(In a clothes shop)

Laura: What would you like to buy, Hiroko?
Hiroko: Well, I'd like to buy something to wear in the dormitory.
Laura: Really? Like what?
Hiroko: Yeah, I'm thinking of getting a pair of training pants. Because they'll be comfortable in the dormitory.
Laura: ……. (?????? staring at Hiroko) What?

Q. Why does Laura stare at Hiroko?

A1. Because Hiroko's pronunciation was so terrible that Laura couldn't understand her.
A2. Because Hiroko should not wear such kind of clothes there.
A3. Because Laura thought Hiroko was very humorous.
A4. Because Laura thought that she should tell her where the nearest drugstore is.

異文化理解 おもしろクイズ 17 アメリカ人の知らない英語(3)

Read the following dialogue and answer the question below.

Hiroko is talking with her roommate, Laura, in their room.

Laura: Hiroko, you've been here for one week, haven't you?
Hiroko: Yes. You've been very helpful, Laura. It's very kind of you.
Laura: My pleasure! Your speaking and listening ability is very good.
Hiroko: Really? I'm happy to hear that. I think it is probably because I take a hearing test almost every day.
Laura: A hearing test?
Hiroko: Yes. It seems very effective to me.
Laura: ……..

Q. Laura seems to be a little confused. Why?

A1. Because Hiroko's pronunciation was so terrible that Laura couldn't understand her.
A2. Because Laura worried about Hiroko's handicap.
A3. Because Laura didn't think Hiroko could use English well.

異文化理解 おもしろクイズ 18 アメリカ人の知らない英語(4)

Hiroko and her roommate Laura go shopping downtown. They buy their favorite clothes and something else for winter.

Hiroko: I'm very happy today, because I've bought this pretty muffler. I like this color very much.
Laura: What? What did you say?
Hiroko: This muffler is nice, isn't it?
Laura: Oh! We call it a scarf. A muffler is a part of a car.
Hiroko: Is it? I didn't know that. Thank you very much. You're a very kind teacher of English.
Laura: My pleasure!
Hiroko: By the way, I'm a little hungry. I'd like something sweet.
Laura: Shall we have some crepes or something?
Hiroko: I feel hot, so I'd like to try some soft cream or ice candy. Some cider is all right, too. Look! That decoration cake looks very delicious. Shall we try that?
Laura: Oh, no. Your strange English again!

Q. Correct the parts of Hiroko's English which Laura can't understand into the right words.

| 異文化理解 おもしろクイズ | **19** アメリカ人の知らない英語(5) |

Q1. What do the following sentences mean?

1. He is a man of moods.　　ア．ムードのある人
　　　　　　　　　　　　　イ．気むずかしい人
2. He is a dandy.　　　　　　ア．かっこいい人
　　　　　　　　　　　　　イ．服装にうるさい人
3. He is naïve.　　　　　　　ア．純心で素朴
　　　　　　　　　　　　　イ．世間知らずでだまされやすい
4. She is smart.　　　　　　　ア．スタイル／プロポーションがいい
　　　　　　　　　　　　　イ．あたまがいい
5. She is a glamour girl.　　　ア．魅力的だ
　　　　　　　　　　　　　イ．グラマーだ

Q2. Choose suitable words from the list below.

1. 現代っ子はよくドライだと言われる。
   Young Japanese today are often called (　　).
2. あの先生はとてもシビアだ。
   That teacher is very (　　).
3. 彼ってメジャーだよね。
   He is (　　).
4. 最近，私の上司はいつもヒステリックになっている。
   Recently my boss is always (　　).
5. あなたのチャーム・ポイントは何ですか。
   What is your most (　　) feature?
6. 彼女は洋服のセンスがいい。
   She has good (　　) in clothes.
7. 彼は時間にルーズだ。
   He is not (　　).
8. 君はオーバーだよ。
   You (　　).

```
ア．popular    イ．strict      ウ．businesslike   エ．on edge
オ．taste      カ．attractive  キ．punctual       ク．exaggerate
```

異文化理解 おもしろクイズ 20 ガイジンを悩ませる英語(1)

Japanese people sometimes confuse English-speaking people. (A) is wrong, but Japanese people often use such expressions. (B) is correct. Fill in the blanks, choosing proper words from the list below.

1. レストランで，前のお客さんの食器を片づけてほしいとき
    (A) × Could you clean the table?
    (B) ○ Could you (　　) the table?

2. めでたくご結婚…
    (A) × Jack married with Rose.
    (B) ○ Jack married Rose. または Jack got married (　　) Rose.

3. 私の家はウサギ小屋なの。
    (A) × My house is narrow.
    (B) ○ I live in a (　　) house.

4. 将来の展望があるの！
    (A) × I have a vision.
    (B) ○ I am a person (　　) vision.

5. よくパーカーを着ているよ。
    (A) × He often wears a parka in the classroom.
    (B) ○ He often wears a sweat shirt with a (　　) in the classroom.

ア．clear　イ．small　ウ．hood　エ．to　オ．with

異文化理解 おもしろクイズ 21 ガイジンを悩ませる英語(2)

Q. Choose the correct words.

1. ［店で］ちょっと見ているだけよ。
   I'm (① just looking ／ ② watching around), thank you.

2. ぼくのことを忘れないで！
   Think (① about me ／ ② of me).

3. よろこんで手伝うよ。
   I (① am willing ／ ② will be happy) to help you.

4. サラダを作るわ。
   I'm going to (① cook ／ ② make) a salad.

5. キャッ，恥ずかしい。
   I'm (① so ashamed ／ ② so embarrassed).

6. チーズを切ったよ。
   I (① cut ／ ② sliced) the cheese.

7. 手に取ってみてもいいですか。
   Can I (① pick it up ／ ② take it)?

8. ［電話で］どちらさまですか。
   (① Who's calling? ／ ② Who are you?)

9. 試着させて下さい。
   Can I (① put ／ ② try) this on?

4. 知っておきたい英語の知識

学校英語では，教えてもらえない「英語ならではの表現」を紹介する。また，'ちょっと違い'で'大違い'の注意すべき発音と，案外まちがって理解していることが多い表現を取り上げる。

異文化理解 おもしろクイズ 22　Metaphor

Q. A word or a phrase is sometimes used imaginatively to make the description more forceful and interesting. Join group A and group B.

< A >	< B >
1. Adam's apple	ア．唯一の弱点
2. dog-ear	イ．不器用
3. back-seat-driver	ウ．予想外の競争相手
4. Achilles' heel	エ．とても簡単だ（朝食前だ）
5. dark horse	オ．彼は考えが甘い
6. He is a creampuff.	カ．のどぼとけ
7. He is all thumbs.	キ．本のページの隅折れ
8. That's a piece of cake.	ク．余計な口出しをする人
9. He is a night owl.	ケ．彼は夜型人間だ
10. It's raining cats and dogs.	コ．どしゃ降りだ

| 異文化理解 おもしろクイズ | 23 | **Body** |

Q. A word or a phrase is sometimes used imaginatively to make the descriptions more forceful and interesting. Choose suitable words from the list below.

1. Hold your (　　). 黙れ！
2. He eats out of her (　　). 彼は彼女の言いなりだ。
3. I have no (　　) for figures. 私は数字に弱い。
4. None of your (　　)! 生意気な口をきくな。
5. Keep your (　　) clean. お行儀よくしなさい。
6. She was born with a sweet (　　). 彼女は根っからの甘党だ。
7. He cooled my (　　). 彼は私を長く待たせた。
8. She gave him the cold (　　). 彼女は彼を無視した。
9. I saved my (　　). 私はけがを免れた。
10. I have butterflies in my (　　). 胸騒ぎがする。

ア．tongue　　イ．head　　ウ．nose　　エ．heels　　オ．lips
カ．tooth　　キ．hand　　ク．skin　　ケ．stomach　　コ．shoulder

| 異文化理解 おもしろクイズ | 24 | **Colors** |

Jane is an exchange student from the U.S. She's staying with Hiromi's family. Jane and Hiromi are watching TV now.

Jane:　　Look! Look at the weather forecast. There are a lot of red suns on the map.

Hiromi:　Yes, it will be fine tomorrow all over Japan.

Jane:　　I see, but we usually use yellow when we paint a picture of the sun. The sun doesn't look red, does it?

Hiromi:　I know, but …

Jane:　　I've never thought that people have different ideas about the color

	of the sun. In Japan do you use red for the sun?
Hiromi:	Sure. Yellow is the color for the moon.
Jane:	That's interesting. I use white for the moon.
Hiromi:	Really? We have different ways of seeing colors, don't we?
Jane:	Yes. Talking of colors, we have various expressions with colors. Look at these. What do you think they mean?

Q. Try to fill in the blanks.

1	blue film	ポルノ映画
2	( ) Monday	憂鬱な月曜日
3	blue lady	才女
4	( )-pencil	文章を修正する
5	green table	賭博台 [英]，会議用テーブル [米]
6	greenbacks	ドル札
7	( )-handed	現行犯の
8	white lie	罪のないうそ
9	white elephant	無用の長物（役に立たないもの）
10	black sheep	厄介者
11	( ) tea	紅茶
12	black gold	石油
13	black art	魔法
14	I'm in the ( ).	健康だ
15	He is ( ).	臆病者だ
16	He is green.	未熟者だ
17	She married into ( ).	玉の輿に乗った
18	He has green fingers.	園芸がうまい

25

異文化理解 おもしろクイズ 25　アメリカ英語とイギリス英語(1)

Read the following dialogue and answer the question below.

Yumi is a Japanese student, who has been studying English in London. She is going to meet her host-brother Mike and go sightseeing with him.

(*At the department store*)

Yumi:　Mike! Mike! Over here!

Mike:　Oh, Yumi, I've found you at last! I've been looking for the shoe department on the first floor as you said, but I couldn't find it, so …

Yumi:　Wait a second, Mike. What do you mean?

Mike:　Well, I mean, in my country, this is not the first floor but the ground floor!

Yumi:　Oh, yes! I'm not in Japan any more. I'm very sorry for my mistake, Mike.

Mike:　That's O.K., Yumi. Anyway, why don't we go sightseeing? I'll show you around London.

Yumi:　Great! Where are we going first?

Mike:　Let me see. · First, we'll take the ah … "subway," and …

Yumi:　You mean, we will take the "tube," right?

Mike:　Good on you! <u>You're catching on quickly</u>, Yumi.

Q.　Why did Mike say to Yumi, "<u>You're catching on quickly</u>"?

異文化理解おもしろクイズ 26 アメリカ英語とイギリス英語(2)

Q. 下の語群のアメリカ英語とイギリス英語を区別し、表を完成しなさい。

	意味	アメリカ英語	イギリス英語
1	ズボン	pants	trousers
2	ガソリン	gas / gasoline	petrol
3	手荷物	baggage	luggage
4	地下鉄		
5	エレベーター	elevator	lift
6	アパート	apartment	flat
7	映画		
8	映画館	movie theater	cinema
9	歩道	sidewalk	pavement
10	時刻表	schedule	timetable
11	トラック	truck	lorry
12	バス		
13	紙幣	bill	note / bank note
14	ピーマン	bell pepper	green pepper
15	ポテトチップス		
16	フライドポテト	French fries	chips
17	ビスケット	cracker	biscuit
18	1階		
19	サッカー		
20	列	line	queue

(soccer / football) (coach / bus) (film / movie)
(subway / underground) (crisps / potato chips) (first floor / ground floor)

| 異文化理解 おもしろクイズ | 27 | L & R (1) |

Q. Linda, an exchange student from America, inclines her head to one side when listening to Hiroko's speech. Why? Pay attention to the underlined words.

Hiroko is a 15-year-old girl, who goes to junior high school in Shimizu. She made a speech about her family today.

Hiroko said:

These days my elder brother is studying very hard to prepare for the entrance exams to university, and <u>reads</u> the columns of newspapers every day. My parents hope that he will have the <u>courage</u> to try some famous universities. But his <u>rate</u> of success will be very low. My brother doesn't seem to have confidence. <u>Right</u> answers will probably help him succeed. On the other hand, <u>wrong</u> answers will prevent him from passing the exams. Anyway I'd like him to become a <u>freshman</u> at a university. And I want to see my kind brother relaxed.

異文化理解おもしろクイズ 28　L & R (2)

Q. Be careful when you pronounce the following words. Match the pairs from the list A and B, and fill the blanks with the correct words.

< A >

1	alive / arrive
2	/ courage
3	lead / read
4	light /
5	play / pray
6	lice / rice
7	law / raw
8	flee / free
9	glamour / grammar
10	climb / crime
11	flesh / fresh
12	late / rate
13	long /
14	bloom / broom
15	list /
16	lack / rack
17	lane / / rain
18	fly / fry

< B >

ア	肉 / 新鮮な
イ	光 / 正しい
ウ	車線 / lieの過去分詞 / 雨
エ	長い / 誤った
オ	しらみ / 米
カ	リスト / 手首
キ	大学 / 勇気
ク	遅い / 割合
ケ	導く / 読む
コ	法律 / なまの
サ	不足 / 棚
シ	花が咲く / ほうき
ス	遊ぶ / 祈る
セ	のみ / 逃げる / 自由な
ソ	魅力 / 文法
タ	飛ぶ / 揚げる
チ	登る / 罪
ツ	生きている / 到着する

— 29 —

異文化理解 おもしろクイズ 29 Misleading Pronunciation

<Pair Work>　Which word did your partner read?

1		7	
pin	pen	can't	count
2		8	
hat	heart	all doctors	old doctors
3		9	
pen	pan	mouse	mouth
4		10	
long	wrong	sheep	ship
5		11	
pull	pool	mummy	money
6		12	
cart	card	fox	forks

異文化理解 おもしろクイズ 30 will と be going to

Read the following dialogue and answer the question below.

Akiko and David are working for a trade company in Yokohama. They are good friends and sometimes have a date these days.

(Around 5:00)
David: Why don't you have dinner with me and go to the movies?
Akiko: Sorry, David. I can't have dinner with you this evening.
David: Can I ask why?
Akiko: Of course. I will eat with Tom.
David: Oh … You will …

Q. David looks a little shocked. Why?

A1. Because David doesn't like Tom.
A2. Because David thinks Akiko has come to like Tom better.
A3. Because David doesn't understand what Akiko said.

5. 英語の「構え」でコミュニケーション

英語でコミュニケーションを図るときは，アイ・コンタクト，ジェスチャーなどのノン・バーバルな要素も含め，英語の「構え」が肝心。英会話は言葉のキャッチ・ボールと言うが，言葉だけでなく，身体のいろいろな部分を総動員したやりとりで「心の通じるコミュニケーション活動」ができるのが望ましい。柔らかな心と頭でLet's try!

異文化理解 おもしろクイズ 31　Gestures (1)

Q. Read the dialogue and choose the gestures to match the meaning of the underlined expressions.

Mary: Hi, Lisa. How was the test last week?
Lisa: The test? ₁No good! How about you, Mary?
Mary: ₂I did pretty well. I got much better marks than before. When I told my mother about it, ₃she looked so surprised.
Lisa: I envy you. ₄My father got angry with me.
Mary: Well … we'll have another test next Monday. Why don't you do your best? ₅Good luck!
Lisa: Thanks. I'll try.
Mary: You can do it!

異文化理解 おもしろクイズ 32

Gestures (2)

Q. What do these gestures mean? Choose suitable meanings from the list below. Then compare your gestures with Western ones.

ア．crazy
イ．I don't know.
ウ．I don't think so.
エ．I, me
オ．money
カ．I made a mistake.
キ．Come here.
ク．I did it!
ケ．I'm thinking.
コ．Silly you!（アッカンベー）

異文化理解 おもしろクイズ 33 同意の合いの手

Fill in the blanks with suitable expressions from the list below.

Judy: Japanese food is very healthy, isn't it?
You: _____1_____

Judy: American food is very rich, so many people get fat.
You: _____2_____

Judy: Would you take me to a Japanese restaurant?
You: _____3_____

Judy: I'd like to try sushi. Is it tasty?
You: _____4_____

Judy: I hear Uogashi-zushi is a good place. Is it true?
You: _____5_____

> ア．I see.　　イ．Exactly.　　ウ．Oh, yes.
> エ．Sure.　　オ．That's right.

異文化理解 おもしろクイズ 34 うながす合いの手

Fill in the blanks with suitable expressions from the list below.

Karen: First, we have to review the schedule of the trip.
Emily: _____1_____

Karen: Then we should think about the cost.
Emily: _____2_____

Karen: It is important for us to visit a lot of museums.
Emily: _____3_____

Karen: We'd also like to enjoy shopping.
Emily: _____4_____

Karen: Of course, we'll enjoy delicious food in every place we visit.

ア．Uh-huh.　　イ．What else?　　ウ．And then?
エ．Go on.　　オ．And ...?

― 35

異文化理解 おもしろクイズ 35　驚きの合いの手

Make the conversation sound natural using expressions from the list below.

Karen: My 78-year-old grandmother started swimming recently.
Emily: _____1_____

Karen: She can swim in any style. She loves freestyle best.
Emily: _____2_____

Karen: She often goes on a hike with her friends.
Emily: _____3_____

Karen: And most of her friends are not female but male.
Emily: _____4_____

Karen: One of them proposed to her and she accepted the proposal.
Emily: _____5_____

ア．Really?
イ．I can't believe it.
ウ．Unbelievable. / Incredible.
エ．What?
オ．You're kidding! / No kidding!
カ．Amazing.
キ．That's a surprise.

| 異文化理解 おもしろクイズ | 36 | **Come On** |

Read the following dialogue and answer the question below.

Keiko is a Japanese student, who is staying with Mr. and Mrs. Ford. She is chatting with her host sisters, Anne and Sandy, in the living room after dinner.

Sandy: My favorite TV program <u>comes on</u> at eight this evening.
Anne: <u>Come on</u>, Sandy. It's a horror film, isn't it? I don't like it. I'd like to watch the football game then.
Sandy: Don't say that, please. The film is very thrilling. Let's watch it together. <u>Come on</u>, Anne.

Sandy turns on the TV and begins watching the horror film.

Anne: <u>Come on</u>, Sandy. You watched it last week. It is my turn.
Mrs. Ford: <u>Come on</u>, both of you. Stop quarreling. <u>Come</u> and help me with the washing up.

Q. Keiko looks confused. Why?

| 異文化理解 おもしろクイズ | 37 How Can I Answer It? |

Western people living in Japan are sometimes asked strange questions, and they are confused by them.

Q. Link the situations to the expressions foreign people sometimes feel a little strange about. Try to think about the reason why these communication gaps occur.

1. 日本に到着したばかりの外国人に
2. 親しくなってきた外国人に
3. 「タテマエ」って何ですかと尋ねた外国人に対して
4. 仕事上のパーティーを無事終えたときに
5. 日本企業への就職試験に合格した外国人に

ア．What is your blood type?
イ．Maybe you can't understand it, because you are not Japanese.
ウ．How lucky you are!
エ．What is your first impression of Japan?
オ．You must be tired.

They feel confused when Japanese people ask these questions of them.

1. Is your wife/husband Japanese?
2. How long have you been married?
3. Why did you come to Japan?
4. How long have you lived in Japan?
5. What does your father do?

異文化理解おもしろクイズ 38 Small Talk (1)

Q. Do you know what small talk is? Small talk helps you avoid remaining silent and make conversation with someone you don't know smooth and happy. Which expressions do you think are suitable as an opening comment when you meet a person for the first time?

1. It's a good party, isn't it?
2. How old are you?
3. Is the weather always this good in November?
4. You don't look well. What's wrong with you?
5. What line of work are you in?
6. What's it like being a journalist?
7. Do you make a lot of money?
8. Where did you buy that tie?
9. The food is delicious, isn't it?
10. Are you from around here?
11. It's a beautifully decorated room, isn't it?
12. Where's your wife?

| 異文化理解 おもしろクイズ 39 | **Small Talk (2)** |

Which expression do you think is suitable in each case?

(1) パーティーで初対面の女性に
  1. I like your dress.
  2. Great party, isn't it?
  3. How much did you pay for those shoes?

(2) バスの中で疲れた様子の老人に会ったとき
  1. May I hold your shopping bags?
  2. Would you like to sit down?
  3. You look tired. Sit down.

(3) バーで誰かと話を始めたいと思ったとき
  1. Who are you?
  2. Hi! Do you come here very often?
  3. It sure is hot today.

(4) パーティーで外国人に会ったとき
  1. Are you an American?
  2. Can you eat Japanese food?
  3. Is this the first time you've been here?

(5) 会社で新入社員に話しかけるとき
  1. Hi, my name's Peter. Let me know if there's anything I can help you with.
  2. Are you new? Where do you work?
  3. Where did you work before joining this company?

(6) エレベーターで外国人と乗り合わせたとき
  1. Nice to meet you.
  2. Why are you in Japan?
  3. This is a slow elevator, isn't it?

6. 生活文化から生じるコミュニケーション・ギャップ

ちょっとした生活習慣の違いから思いもよらぬ勘違いが生じることがある。双方の文化を理解した上で対話を進めたり，日本の文化について紹介できるとよい。

異文化理解 おもしろクイズ 40　Souvenirs

Read the following dialogue and answer the question below.

Mr. White has recently come to Japan. He visits Mr. Kato's house for the first time.

Mr. White:　Good afternoon, Mr. Kato.
Mr. Kato:　Good afternoon, Mr. White.
Mr. White:　Thank you for inviting me to your place. This is for you. (handing him a small present)
Mr. Kato:　Thank you. (bowing)

Mr. Kato takes the present into another room, without saying anything, comes back and continues to talk.

Mr. Kato:　How was your flight?
Mr. White:　Oh … yeah. It was nice.

Q. Mr. White looks a little uneasy, even disappointed. Why?

A1.　Mr. White sat on tatami, and his feet became numb.

A2.　Mr. White has heard that giving a present is very important in Japan, and he was worried that Mr. Kato was not pleased with the present.

A3.　Mr. White has only learned a little Japanese before he came to Japan. So he was at a loss what to say.

A4.　Mr. White could not make himself at home, because he thought Japanese custom was too strict.

異文化理解 おもしろクイズ 41 Toilet

Read the following dialogue and answer the question below.

Mr. White has come to Japan on business. He was invited to a Japanese house.

Mr. White: Excuse me, may I use the bathroom?
Mrs. Kato: Yes, of course. Come this way.

But Mr. White came back to the living room quickly.

Mr. White: Excuse me, but do you happen to have another bathroom?
Mrs. Kato: I'm sorry, but we don't have a western toilet.
Mr. White: Oh … (puzzled) It is no problem, but …

Q.   What do you think is Mr. White's problem?

| 異文化理解 おもしろクイズ | 42 | **Guest** |

Read the following dialogue and answer the question below.

Mrs. Suzuki has lived in America for three months. Today she invites her new friend, Mrs. Smith. This is the first time for Mrs. Smith to visit Mrs. Suzuki.

Mrs. Smith:　　Good afternoon.
Mrs. Suzuki:　　Good afternoon.
Mrs. Smith:　　Thank you for inviting me.
Mrs. Suzuki:　　Not at all.
Mrs. Smith:　　What a lovely house you have!
Mrs. Suzuki:　　Oh, no! It is very old.
　　　　　　　　Please have a seat.
　　　　　　　　Make yourself at home.

Mrs. Suzuki goes into the kitchen and prepares tea. Mrs. Smith gets up from her seat, and comes into the kitchen.

Mrs. Smith:　　Is there anything I can do to help?
Mrs. Suzuki:　　Oh, nothing. Please have a seat and just relax. I'll be there in a moment.
Mrs. Smith:　　……..

Q. Mrs. Smith seems to be waiting for something. What would she like to do?

A1.　She would like to go to the bathroom.
A2.　She would like to eat something. She is hungry.
A3.　She would like to look around Mrs. Suzuki's house.

異文化理解 おもしろクイズ	43	**Tea Time**

Read the following dialogue and answer the question below.

Two weeks later, Mrs. Smith invites Mrs. Suzuki to her house. Mrs. Suzuki visits Mrs. Smith for the first time.

Mrs. Smith: I'm so glad you could visit me today. I know you are busy.
Mrs. Suzuki: Thank you for your kind invitation.
Mrs. Smith: Please come into the kitchen while I fix us a drink. Would you like coffee or tea?
Mrs. Suzuki: Anything will do.
Mrs. Smith: Oh, everything is easy. Besides coffee or tea, I have juice or coke.
Mrs. Suzuki: Well, whatever you are having is fine.
Mrs. Smith: Well, are you sure? I'm going to have tea. Is that all right?
Mrs. Suzuki: Yes.
Mrs. Smith: How would you like your tea? With sugar, honey, cream, or lemon?
Mrs. Suzuki: Just as it is please.
Mrs. Smith: How about some cookies? I baked some this morning. Or maybe some strawberries?
Mrs. Suzuki: Either would be lovely.
Mrs. Smith: Well then, we'll have both. Here, would you mind taking these strawberries? I'll be right there with the tea and cookies.

Q. What does Mrs. Smith think about Mrs. Suzuki's attitude?

Mrs. Smith thinks Mrs. Suzuki is (ア. shy, イ. embarrassed, ウ. polite, エ. impolite, オ. indecisive, カ. friendly). And why?

44 In the Classroom

Q. Read the following dialogue and answer the questions below.

Ms. Green is a new ALT (assistant language teacher), who has come from America. She was sent to Shizuoka prefecture to teach senior high school students. Today is the first day of teaching English.

Ms. Green: Good morning. Nice to meet you.
Students: Good morning.
Ms. Green: Let me introduce myself. My name is Juliet Green. I come from Boston, U.S.A. I majored in European history and French. I like swimming, jogging and reading. Do you know a good place for swimming around here?
Students: (Silent)
Ms. Green: Can you hear me? Please tell me a good place for swimming.
Students: (Silent, looking at each other)
Ms. Green: O.K. So you don't have a swimming pool around here. Then I'd like to ask about your hobbies. What's your hobby? Come on. Anyone can answer.
Students: (Silent. Some are looking down at the textbooks, and some are smiling slightly.)

Q. What do you think of the Japanese students' attitude?
What does Ms. Green think of Japanese students?

異文化理解 おもしろクイズ 45 In the Teachers' Room

Read the following dialogue and answer the question below.

Ms. Green, an assistant language teacher, has just started teaching at a senior high school in Shizuoka. She comes to the teacher's room around 8:00 in the morning.

Ms. Green: Good morning, Mr. Kato.
Mr. Kato: Good morning, Ms. Green.
Ms. Green: Oh! What a nice tie! You look so cool.
Mr. Kato: (becomes red) You must be kidding.
Ms. Green: No, not at all. I'm serious. You look really cool.
Mr. Kato: This tie is very cheap. It is not a good one.
Ms. Green: It's very good. It must be expensive.
Mr. Kato: (confused) ……..

Q. Do you often compliment your friends, family, and so on?

異文化理解 おもしろクイズ	46	**Hiccups**

Read the following dialogue and answer the question below.

Tom and Ken are high school students in Salt Lake City. Ken approaches Tom on tiptoe from behind and surprises him.

Ken: Wa!
Tom: Ouch! Why did you do that? You made me bite my tongue. Look! It's bleeding.
Ken: Oh, sorry. I just wanted to help you stop your hiccups.
Tom: I was trying to stop them, too.
Ken: How?
Tom: I was counting up to ten with my tongue stuck out.
Ken: Wow! That sounds hard to do. Does it work? In Japan we surprise people to stop their hiccups.
Tom: Hey, my hiccups stopped! Which way do you think worked?

Q. How do you usually stop hiccups? Does it work well?

<Notes>
hiccup [híkʌp] = しゃっくり（通例 ～s で単数扱い）

異文化理解 おもしろクイズ 47 — Nodding

Read the following dialogue and answer the question below.

Mr. Saito is a Japanese businessman, who has just started working at a branch office in Los Angeles. He is shopping for domestic items. He is talking with a salesman, Mark. Mark is explaining how to use a fan heater.

Mark: Let me explain first how to use this machine, O.K.?
Mr. Saito: (Nods.) Yes.
Mark: Press this button and the machine starts to operate.
Mr. Saito: (Nods.) Yes.
Mark: Set the self-timer and it will stop automatically.
Mr. Saito: (Nods.) Yes.
Mark: You can take the machine home with you today and pay later.
Mr. Saito: (Nods.) Yes.
Mark: O.K., so go ahead and fill out this form and sign here.
Mr. Saito: Sorry, I don't want it.
Mark: What? But you've been nodding and saying "yes"! I thought you were going to buy it.
Mr. Saito: No, I was just listening.
Mark: Goodness gracious!

Q. What has made Mark misunderstand?

| 異文化理解 おもしろクイズ | 48 | **The Japanese Smile** |

Read the following dialogue and answer the question below.

Taro is a Japanese student, who has been studying business at UCLA for three months. He is going to the movies with Linda.

(In front of the theater)

Linda: I wonder what happened to him? I've been waiting for more than an hour!

Taro: Hi, Linda. Sorry to be late. I overslept. (Smiles wryly.)

Linda: You've kept me waiting more than one hour!

Taro: It's so cold, you know, it took me a while to get the engine started, ha ha …

Linda: What's so funny? I'm mad!

Taro: I know. That's why I said, "I'm sorry." (With a big smile.)

Linda: What are you still smiling for?

Taro: Oh, I am? I wasn't aware of that.

Q. What has got Linda so angry?

異文化理解 おもしろクイズ 49 — Either Will Do

Read the following dialogue and answer the question below.

Taro is a Japanese student, who has been studying business at UCLA for three months. He goes to the movies with Linda. After watching a film, they have supper.

(In front of the theater)

Linda: That was a funny movie, wasn't it? I'm starving. Let's have supper. Which do you feel like eating, Chinese or Western food?

Taro: Either will do.

Linda: Well, let's have Western then. Which do you want, French or Italian food?

Taro: Well, either would be fine.

Linda: Let's have Italian, then. (They enter the restaurant and are seated.) What do you want to drink, wine or beer?

Taro: Anything will do.

Linda: Let's have some wine, shall we? So what do you want to order, Taro?

Taro: Well, anything will be OK.

Q. How does Linda feel about Taro's attitude?

A1. She is angry.

A2. She is irritated.

A3. She is surprised.

A4. She is disappointed.

異文化理解 おもしろクイズ	50	**Etiquette**

Read the following dialogue and answer the question below.

John is an American student, who has been studying business at Shizuoka University for three months. He and his friend Ichiro are going to have lunch.

John: I'm hungry. Why don't we have lunch? I'd like to try some Japanese food.

Ichiro: We ate *sushi* the other day. How about *soba*, today?

John: That sounds good. Let's go.

(At a noodle restaurant close to the university)

John: Listen! What a lot of noise that guy makes when he eats!

Ichiro: In Japan it's OK to make a noise when you eat noodles, but not other dishes.

John: That reminds me. In Arabian countries it's good manners to burp when you've finished your meals, I heard. Customs differ from country to country.

Ichiro: So many countries, so many customs, we also say.

John: (Takes out a handkerchief.)

Q. What do you imagine John does next?

A1. He goes to the bathroom.

A2. He wipes the table.

A3. He blows his nose, making a loud noise.

A4. He wipes the sweat on the forehead.

| 異文化理解 おもしろクイズ | 51 | **Invitation** |

Read the following dialogue and answer the question below.

Mr. Brown is a businessman working for an American trade company. He has been working at the Tokyo branch for three months. Mr. Nakamura, his colleague, has just bought a new house.

Mr. Brown: Hi, Mr. Nakamura. What are you going to have for lunch?
Mr. Nakamura: I'd like to have *katsudon*.
Mr. Brown: It sounds delicious. May I join you?
Mr. Nakamura: Yes, of course.
(At the Japanese restaurant)
Mr. Brown: I heard you've bought a house at last.
Mr. Nakamura: Yes. I decided to do it finally.
Mr. Brown: I know houses are very expensive in Japan.
Mr. Nakamura: That's right. So I gave up trying to get a house with a yard, and I chose an apartment instead.
Mr. Brown: Anyway, you must be happy now.
Mr. Nakamura: Yes! Please drop in at my house sometime.
Mr. Brown: Oh, I will, thank you. When would be convenient for you?
Mr. Nakamura: Well, let's see ……….

Q. Mr. Nakamura looks a little confused. Can you imagine why?

| 異文化理解 おもしろクイズ 52 | Family |

Q. How do your family usually talk about your own family members? Choose acceptable expressions.

1. My husband is very sweet and always calls me "Honey."
2. My husband seldom smiles and only says, "I'll take a bath" and "I'll have a meal."
3. My wife is a very cute and considerate person. I love her.
4. Is my wife a wonderful woman? No, not a bit of it. She only thinks of herself.
5. My daughter is a real sweetie.
6. My daughter is not bright. She seldom follows my advice.
7. My son is very smart and a good athlete.
8. My son is only crazy about soccer and studies very little.
9. My mother is a good cook and she is very kind to everyone.
10. My mother is always complaining about my faults. I don't like her.

Please write about your family.

7. 知っておきたい一般知識

年中行事やちょっとした生活様式の違い，英米人なら誰でも知っている基礎知識を取り上げる。さ〜て，どのくらい知っているかな？

異文化理解 おもしろクイズ 53　Halloween

Q. Circle your choices.

1. Halloween is celebrated on _____.
    a. February 14th　　　b. July 14th
    c. October 31st　　　d. December 25th
2. The word comes from medieval England's All Hallows' _____.
    a. eve　　b. time　　c. month　　d. rite
3. _____ are malevolent, evil creatures that fly on broomsticks.
    a. Wizards　　b. Witches　　c. Fairies　　d. Ghosts
4. _____ and black are colors associated with Halloween.
    a. Blue　　b. Red　　c. Orange　　d. Green
5. _____ are carved into jack-o'-lanterns.
    a. Pumpkins　　b. Melons　　c. Potatoes　　d. Onions
6. Children wear scary _____.
    a. habits　　b. costumes　　c. gowns　　d. customs
7. When children go to someone's door they say "_____."
    a. Trick or treat　　　b. Treat or trick
    c. Treat or treat　　　d. Trick or beat
8. _____ are also associated with Halloween.
    a. Black dogs　　　b. Brown bears
    c. Black cats　　　d. White cats

54 Christmas

Q. Answer the questions.

<Santa Claus Quiz>

1. What color is Santa's suit?
2. What is Santa's lead reindeer called?
3. What do the reindeer pull for Santa Claus?
4. What color are Santa's boots?
5. How does Santa get into the house?
6. What does Santa carry the toys in?
7. What do children hang up for Santa to put the toys in?

<Christmas Tradition Quiz>

1. What bird is cooked for Christmas dinner?
2. Where are the presents kept before opening them?
3. What is hung outside on the door?
4. Before electricity, what were put on the trees?
5. What is a common four letter abbreviation of Christmas?
6. What plant with red berries is used for decorations?
7. What do you kiss under?

<Christmas Story Quiz>

1. How many wise men were there?
2. Where did Mary and Joseph have to sleep?
3. What did the wise men follow?
4. What did Mary ride on?
5. What was Joseph's job?
6. What city did Joseph and Mary go to?
7. Who were watching the sheep?

| 異文化理解 おもしろクイズ | 55 | **Traffic Signs** |

Q. Are these signs American or Japanese? What are they called? Can you find any difference between the two signs? And why?

A   B   A   B

| 異文化理解 おもしろクイズ | 56 | **Emergency** |

Read the following dialogue and answer the question below.

Keiko is studying English in Oxford. She is staying with Mr. and Mrs. Jones. She has three housemates, Mary from France, Lisa from Italy and Ran from Korea. They go to the same language school. One afternoon they come home together.

Keiko: Oh, the door is open. I wonder Mrs. Jones is already home.
Mary: Hello. We are home!
(No one answers.)
Lisa: She must be upstairs.
(They go upstairs.)
Ran: Look! What a mess!
Lisa: Oh, no. Someone broke into the house! Call the police!!
Keiko: I'll do it. (She dials.) I can't get them.
Mary: I'll try it. (She dials.) Why can't I get them?
Ran: What are you doing? Give me the phone. (She dials.) Is the phone out of order? I can't get the police.
Lisa: Can I try it? (She dials.) I'm sorry. Me neither.

Q. They can't get the police on the phone. Why?

| 異文化理解 おもしろクイズ | 57 | Oh My God! |

Q. The way of life and the use of languages have been influenced by Christianity. A lot of English-speaking people respect and believe in God, but they sometimes use these words impolitely. Choose suitable meanings from the list below.

1	Jesus Christ	
2	For Christ sake	何てこった
3	Hell	ちぇっ
4	Damn（他動詞：神が罰する）	こん畜生
5	For God's sake	お願いだから
6	For heaven's sake	お願いだから
7	Good Heavens	困った
8	Oh my God	何たることだ
9	My goodness (=God)	何たることだ
10	Gosh (=God)	
11	By Gosh／By God	本当に，まさか，とんでもない
12	Good Lord!／Oh Lord!	おやまあ，とんでもない
13	Go to hell!	
14	What the hell!	かまうもんか，どうでもいいや
15	God in Heaven!	くそ！ なんてこった

　　ア．おやまあ　　　イ．こん畜生，バカ野郎　　　ウ．くたばってしまえ

要注意！　This kind of expression is often used and you will hear it in movies etc. but they are very difficult to use naturally, especially for non-native speakers. Try to understand them, but don't use them!

異文化理解 おもしろクイズ 58 Who Are These People?

Q. Who are these people?   Use the box below to write your choices.

1. The Black Civil Rights leader who fought segregation through nonviolent protests. Awarded the 1964 Nobel Peace Prize.
2. The Hindu nationalist and spiritual leader who was assassinated in 1948.
3. Born in 1917, he was the 35th President of the USA. He was assassinated in 1963.
4. The American statesman, author and scientist. His many inventions included the lightning rod and bifocal glasses.
5. The Famous American novelist who became the 5th American to receive the Nobel Prize for literature. *For Whom the Bell Tolls* (1940) is considered by many his finest novel.
6. A Jewish girl. She wrote in her diary, which recorded the experiences of her family living for two years in hiding from the Nazis in occupied Amsterdam.
7. A Roman Catholic nun. She founded the Missionaries of Charity in India, which became noted for its work among the poor. She won the Nobel Peace Prize in 1979.
8. The Black leader who fought against apartheid in South Africa. He became a symbol for equal rights and justice.

```
ア．Nelson Mandela
イ．Benjamin Franklin
ウ．Mahatma Gandhi
エ．Mother Teresa
オ．John F. Kennedy
カ．Martin Luther King, Jr.
キ．Ernest Hemingway
ク．Anne Frank
```

異文化理解 おもしろクイズ 59 Witty Remarks

Q. Who said these famous words? Choose people from the list below.

1. Boys, be ambitious.
2. The government of the people, by the people and for the people.
3. I am the state.
4. Yet the earth moves.
5. Man is a thinking reed.
6. Genius is one per cent inspiration and ninety-nine per cent perspiration.
7. You, too, Brutus!
8. Time is money.
9. The word "impossible" is not in my dictionary.
10. I think, therefore I am.

ア．Abraham Lincoln (1809-1865)　第16代米国大統領。奴隷開放宣言。
イ．Benjamin Franklin (1706-1790)　米国の政治家。独立宣言を起草。
ウ．William Smith Clark (1826-1886)　札幌農学校初代教頭。
エ．René Descartes (1596-1650)　フランスの哲学者・数学者。
オ．Louis XIV (1638-1715)　フランス国王。ベルサイユ宮殿を建設。
カ．Thomas Alva Edison (1847-1931)　米国の発明家。蓄音機などを発明。
キ．Blaise Pascal (1623-1662)　フランスの数学者・思想家。
ク．Gaius Julius Caesar (100 B.C.-44 B.C.)　ローマの将軍・政治家。
ケ．Galileo Galilei (1564-1642)　イタリアの天文学者。
コ．Napoleon Bonaparte (1769-1821)　フランス皇帝。

1	2	3	4	5	6	7	8	9	10

| 異文化理解 おもしろクイズ | 60 Quiz about the USA |

Q. Circle your choices.

1. What are the two major parties in the US?
   a. The Republicans and the Democrats
   b. The Republics and the Socialists
   c. The Democrats and the Socialists
   d. The Conservationists and the Democrats

2. How many states are there in the US?
   a. 49   b. 50   c. 51   d. 48

3. What do Americans celebrate on July 4th?
   a. Flag Day   b. The Revolution
   c. The Discovery of America   d. Independence Day

4. In which year was independence from England declared?
   a. 1776   b. 1876   c. 1676   d. 1778

5. Which president freed the slaves?
   a. Thomas Jefferson   b. George Washington
   c. Abraham Lincoln   d. Henry Ford

6. Who was the civil rights leader who fought through nonviolent action?
   a. Thomas Paine   b. Martin Luther King, Jr.   c. John F. Kennedy

7. Who was the first person to walk on the moon?
   a. John Glenn   b. Jim Lowell   c. Neil Armstrong

8. What was the name of the first ship that sailed to America?
   a. The Pitta   b. The Sunflower   c. The Mayflower

9. Where's the White House located?
   a. In New York   b. In Washington, D.C.   c. In Houston

10. What organization tries to find solutions to world problems and disputes?
    a. The United Nations   b. IMF   c. UNICEF   d. Greenpeace

| 異文化理解 おもしろクイズ | 61 | **Quiz about the UK** |

Q. Circle your choices.

1. What is the Queen's name?
   a. Queen Ann I   b. Queen Elizabeth II   c. Queen Margaret II

2. Where does the Changing of the Guard take place?
   a. Buckingham Palace
   b. Piccadilly Circus
   c. Victoria and Albert Museum

3. What is a double-decker?
   a. A bus   b. A disco   c. A taxi

4. What is Harrods?
   a. A bank   b. A department store   c. A school

5. How many pence are there in 1 pound?
   a. 10   b. 100   c. 1,000

6. Which Liverpool band was so popular in the 60s?
   a. The Beatles
   b. The Police
   c. The Rolling Stones

7. Where is Nessie supposed to live?
   a. Isle of Man   b. Loch Ness   c. River Thames

8. In Britain, cars are driven on the _____ side of the road.
   a. left-hand   b. right-hand   c. wrong-hand

9. Dame Agatha Christie wrote lots of _____.
   a. detective stories   b. plays   c. poems

10. Which famous writer was born in Stratford-upon-Avon?
    a. Samuel Beckett
    b. James Joyce
    c. William Shakespeare

| 異文化理解 おもしろクイズ | 62 | **A Rolling Stone** |

Read the following dialogue and answer the question below.

Kazuo has been working for a company in Los Angeles for almost a year. He is chatting with his friends Bill and Lucy at the coffee shop.

Bill: How is it going, Lucy?
Lucy: I'd like to say everything is all right, but I have some trouble.
Kazuo: What's the matter?
Lucy: I'm working hard and I often offer a good idea to my boss.
Bill: I know you're a very good worker.
Kazuo: I think so, too.
Lucy: Thank you, but my boss will never listen to my opinions.
Kazuo: It can sometimes happen. It takes you some time to become used to a new company.
Bill: But I think you can insist what you believe is right.
Lucy: That's true. I want to have my opinion accepted more.
Kazuo: Do you think so? If I were you, I would try to be more patient. The proverb says a rolling stone gathers no moss.
Lucy: What? I can't understand you. That's why I'd like to quit my job and move to another company.

Q. What is the meaning of the proverb to Lucy?

A1. It has the same meaning as *three years on a stone*.
A2. It means aggressive and active persons are great.
A3. It means a person can't save money if he changes his job often.
A4. It means a person can't get true love if he likes many women.

異文化理解 おもしろクイズ 63

Proverbs

Q. Which proverbs come from typical Japanese values?
Which from typical Western values?

1	Nails that stick out get hammered down.
2	Strike while the iron is hot.
3	Patience is a remedy for every sorrow.
4	Never put off till tomorrow what you can do today.
5	Where there's a will, there's a way.
6	Put a lid on smelly things.
7	Every dog has his day.
8	Better late than never.
9	Bound by long twine it's better not to resist.
10	Everything comes to the person who waits.
11	It's better not to know some things.
12	God helps those who help themselves.
13	Knowledge is power.

8. 異文化間に生じる諸問題を考えよう！

文化の違いに対し，柔軟な姿勢を持ち，「へぇ〜そうなんだぁ！」と思う気持ちがあれば，知識も興味関心も実体験も広がっていく。一方，自らの文化や価値観に固執し，異なったものに対して，ある「決め付け」をすると，自分の世界が広がらない。時には，摩擦や衝突が生まれる。この章は「文明の衝突」の世紀を生きぬく皆さんへのメッセージでもある。

異文化理解 おもしろクイズ 64　ALTs from the USA

Look at the pictures and answer the question below.

A Language Camp is held at the foot of Mt. Fuji every summer. This year 7 American teachers help the students use English in their own ways. Today a farewell party is being held and some of the teachers are coming to the party, dressed in their ethnic costumes.

Q. The students seem a little confused to see them. Why?

異文化理解 おもしろクイズ 65 Vegetable Soup

Read the following sentences and choose suitable words from below.

Until the 1960s, immigrants tried to learn English and to make themselves Americanized. Different peoples seemed to be willing to throw away their own identities and assimilate themselves into American society. The phenomenon was called (1).

Through the Civil Rights Movement, people came to identify themselves as Ethnic Groups having their own culture, religion and traditions. They appeared to be unwilling to adapt themselves wholly to the American way of life.

Since 1965, a large percentage of new immigrants have been Asians and Latin Americans. It was called the New Wave of Immigrants. Rather than a (1), American society is now more often compared to a (2). Although many ingredients are mixed together in a (2), each individual ingredient still remains distinctive. American people would like to live together in harmony without losing their cultural identities.

But some say this salad is going bad because the dressing isn't poured evenly all over. A recent, more accurate picture of American society might be imagined as a (3), where pieces of vegetables (= 4) add to the taste but hardly ever become one with the soup (= 5).

　　ア．cultures　　　イ．vegetable soup　　ウ．salad bowl
　　エ．a melting pot　オ．the society

1	2	3	4	5

異文化理解 おもしろクイズ 66 PC (= Politically Correct)

Noriko, who is leaving for America to study English, is talking with her English teacher, Ms. Green, at Narita Airport.

Q1. Choose suitable words from the list below.

Ms. Green: Aren't you nervous, Noriko?
Noriko: Not at all. I like traveling by air. I once wanted to be a stewardess.
Ms. Green: You mean a flight (1).
Noriko: What?
Ms. Green: Well, these days, men and women often do the same jobs, so people prefer to use neutral terms.
Noriko: Like what, for example?
Ms. Green: "(2)" for "chairman," "police (3)" for "policeman," and "fire (4)" for "fireman."
Noriko: I see.

> ア. fighter　　イ. attendant　　ウ. officer　　エ. chairperson

Q2. This is a table about non-PC words and PC words. Fill in the blanks.

non-PC	→	PC
(1)	→	letter carrier or postal worker
wife or (2)	→	spouse　配偶者
(3)	→	salesperson
(4)	→	doorkeeper
Miss, Mrs.	→	(5)
man, mankind	→	people, humanity, human beings, humankind, human species
handicapped	→	physically challenged

異文化理解 おもしろクイズ 67

Stereotypes

Q. What images do foreigners have of the Japanese?
And do you like their images of the Japanese?

	Are the images foreigners have true or not?			Do you like it?	
	True	Not always true	Not true	No problem	I don't like it.
Japanese wear glasses.					
Japanese always carry cameras.					
Japanese are rich.					
Japanese are workaholics.					
Japanese like raw fish.					
Japanese are not creative.					
Japanese have short noses.					
Japanese have short legs.					
Japanese often bow.					

Compare your results with the classmates'. From what or where do you think people get such stereotypes about the Japanese?

異文化理解 おもしろクイズ 68 **Who Are the Japanese?**

Q. Read the following statements. Who do you think is more Japanese? Try to rank the people below from the most Japanese to the least Japanese.

A	I am Eriko. I am fifteen years old. I have a Japanese passport, but I have lived in Thailand with my Japanese parents since I was born. I have been educated in Thailand and I speak Japanese and Thai. I visit Japan to see my grandparents on New Year Days or during the summer holidays.
B	My name is Ellen. I have lived in Japan for sixteen years since I was born in Yokohama. I have been educated in Japanese public schools and I speak fluent Japanese. I don't have a Japanese passport and my parents are not Japanese but Australians.
C	I was born in Paris. My father is Japanese, and my mother is French. My family moved to Japan when I was five. I went to Japanese schools and I speak Japanese and a little French.
D	My great-grand-parents went to Brazil on business. My parents are both Japanese. I was born in Brazil, and was educated there. I speak only Portuguese.
E	I was born in Rome. My father is Italian, and my mother is Japanese. My family moved to Japan when I was four and I was educated in Japanese schools. My eyes are blue, and my hair is fair. I speak Japanese and very little Italian.
F	I was born in New York. My parents are both Japanese. My family came back to Japan when I was six and I was educated in an American school in Tokyo. I speak Japanese and English fluently. I am eighteen years old now. I have just been admitted to a college in Los Angeles. I'd like to get a job there after graduation.

Compare your ranking with that of your classmates.

異文化理解 おもしろクイズ 69 Roots

American society consists of immigrants from all over the world and their descendents. Try to look at their names, and you will often find their races, occupation and their roots.

	Family Names	Roots
1	Washington, Newton	
2	Hansen, Andersen	
3	Johnson, Jackson, Wilson, Robertson, Anderson	
4	McDonald, McGregor, MacArthur, Macbeth	
5	Gladstone, Livingstone	
6	O'Brien, O'Neill, O'Hara	
7	Adams, Jones, Williams, Roberts	
8	Benjamin, Goldsmith, Silverman	

ア．England or Northern Europe
イ．Scotland or Ireland
ウ．England
エ．Jews
オ．Northern Europe
カ．Scotland
キ．Ireland
ク．Wales

異文化理解 おもしろクイズ 70　アメリカ映画の中のニッポン

These are particular scenes from American movies. How are Japanese people shown? Choose how you feel. If you have a chance, try to watch them.

```
ア．funny/humorous      イ．exciting        ウ．realistic
エ．unrealistic          オ．shocking        カ．cynical
```

映画	場　　面	Your Feeling
危険な情事	主人公が妻と共に出席したのは，日本人が書いた『サムライ・セルフ・ヘルプ』という本の出版記念パーティー。著者の日本人はペコペコ何度もお辞儀をしている。	
ティファニーで朝食を	オードリー・ヘップバーンの住むアパートのひとつ上の階に，出っ歯でメガネをかけ，いつも浴衣姿の日本人男性が何度も登場する。	
ミスター・ベースボール	空港に到着。初対面の挨拶はお辞儀の連続。インタビューでは，「日本の印象は？」という質問。来日したばかりで答えようがないので，「空港がきれい」と答える。	
ミスター・ベースボール	球場の控え室。土足禁止，小さいスリッパ，和式トイレ，お風呂の入り方などに戸惑う。日本では「ガイジン」扱いをされると教えられる。	
ミスター・ベースボール	ドリンク剤のコマーシャルに出演。サムライ姿，まわしを締め，力士姿でハイ，ポーズ！	
ミスター・ベースボール	監督の娘と知らず，好意をよせる。休みの日に彼女の家を訪問。出されたそうめんをズルズルとすする。	

メジャーリーグ2	不振のインディアンズに迎えられたのは，サムライ精神の固まり，巨人軍のタナカ選手。紋付き袴で登場。	
ライジング・サン	日本企業が主催するパーティー。和太鼓，和服の日本人女性が人々を迎える。互いにお辞儀の連続。	
	コナー警部の日本解説1。コナー警部が同僚の刑事に日本社会のあり方を説明する場面。「先輩と後輩」の人間関係。	
	殺人現場。日本企業側は「何の関係もございません。」とどこかで聞いたようなセリフで対応。	
	コナー警部の日本解説2。日本企業の特徴。少数の「系列」を支配する巨大な企業グループの存在を説明。	
	容疑者日本人男性。女性の裸体にスシを並べて食べる。	
	コナー警部の日本解説3。「上司の罪は部下がかぶる。」	
ブラック・レイン	ニューヨークのパブ。日本のヤクザが対立するヤクザの首を短刀でかっ切って，偽札の原版を奪う。	
	この殺人の容疑者を追って，ヤクザの事務所へ行くと，出迎えたのは全身入れ墨，フンドシ姿の柄の悪い男達。	
	容疑者を追って大阪へ乗り込んだ刑事2人は，外国人ホステスのいるカラオケ・バーに招かれる。	
	暴走族風のバイクにおびき寄せられた末，刑事の一人チャーリーは日本刀で殺される。	
	容疑者佐藤と対立するヤクザのボス。「太平洋戦争での無念を晴らすためにヤクザをしている」と言う。	

異文化理解 おもしろクイズ 71 映画で学ぶ人権と差別(1)

Q. Fill in the blanks with suitable words.

Do you like movies? I'm sure most of you will say yes! Some of you may be fascinated with brilliant movie stars. Some of you may enjoy unrealistic experiences through computer graphics.

Now I'd like to introduce some good movies to you, but they are not just for fun but for your education.

The themes of the movies are human rights and discrimination. There are a lot of serious issues around the world. One of them is discrimination, which might result from the differences of ①(c-------). People have different ways of life, beliefs and senses of value, which could sometimes result in being ignorant, hating each other, having feelings which in turn lead to quarrels, fights, and wars.

Discrimination occurs because of differences in ②(r---), religion, wealth, intelligence, status, ③(s--), age, occupation, ④(p-------) ability, illness, and so on. If we can ⑤(a-----) different cultures and have open-minded feelings toward them, we may get interested in them and enjoy new ways of life and relationships with new persons.

I hope these movies will help you know about past events and the present situation regarding human rights and discrimination. I hope you will have a wise and flexible mind when you happen to meet cultures different from yours in the future.

異文化理解 おもしろクイズ 72　映画で学ぶ人権と差別(2)

Q. 以下の映画のあらすじを読んで，それぞれのテーマを下から選んで記号で答えなさい。

	Titles & Plots	テーマ
1	*The Color Purple* (1985) A black girl, Celie was treated unfairly and terribly by her own father and her husband. She was made to work as a slave. 主演は『天使にラブ・ソングを…』で有名なウーピー・ゴールドバーグ。監督はスティーヴン・スピルバーグ。	
2	*The Long Walk Home* (1990) The bus boycott in Montgomery. A black woman deliberately chose not to ride on a bus but walk to her job, as a form of non-violent resistance against segregation. ウーピー・ゴールドバーグが白人家庭のメイド役を熱演。	
3	*Schindler's List* (1993) A German businessman, Oscar Schindler, saved more than a thousand Jews from the gas chambers during World War II. 監督・製作はスティーヴン・スピルバーグ。1994年アカデミー賞7部門受賞。白黒の映像が一層胸を打つ。	
4	*Life is Beautiful* (1998) Guido, a Jewish-Italian waiter had a very hard time with his wife and son in a concentration camp, but he had enough wit to cheer his son up in the face of total adversity. 監督・主演は，ロベルト・ベニーニ。独特の哀愁漂う感動作。	
5	*Come See the Paradise* (1990) Japanese-Americans were herded into concentration camps and suffered enormously during World War II. 実話に基づく。邦題は『愛と哀しみの旅路』。	
6	*Philadelphia* (1993) Andrew, a lawyer, lost his job because of his disease (AIDS) and his homosexuality. He fought in the court as his own attorney. 主演はトム・ハンクス。必見の社会派ヒューマンドラマ。	

ア．discrimination against black people　　イ．discrimination against homosexuality
ウ．sexual discrimination　　エ．discrimination against Jewish people
オ．discrimination against Japanese-Americans

異文化理解 おもしろクイズ 73 映画で学ぶ人権と差別(3)

異文化間の摩擦をテーマにした映画を紹介する。一作選んで鑑賞し、感想を150〜200語で書きなさい。

1	アンネの日記 The Diary of Anne Frank 1959年　アメリカ	世界的ベストセラー『アンネの日記』の映画化。ナチスによるユダヤ人の迫害を逃れて屋根裏部屋に暮らす少女とその家族を描く感動作。
2	戦場のピアニスト The Pianist　2002年 ポーランド／フランス	ロマン・ポランスキー監督が、実在のポーランド人ピアニスト、シュピルマンの自伝に、自身のゲットーから脱出し生き延びた過酷な体験を重ね合わせて作った作品。
3	タイタンズを忘れない Remember the Titans 2000年　　アメリカ	奇跡のパワーで快進撃を続けた実在のフットボールチーム"タイタンズ"の実話をもとに、人種問題というテーマを、若者達の青春群像の中でつづった感動作。監督役はデンゼル・ワシントン。
4	ぼくの神さま Edges of the Lord 2000年　アメリカ	ハーレイ・ジョエル・オスメントがナチス占領下のポーランドから逃れるため、農村の一家に匿われたユダヤ人少年を演じた感動作!!
5	評決のとき A Time to Kill 1996年　　アメリカ	娘をレイプした2人の白人を殺した黒人男性、カール・リー。その弁護を引き受けた新米弁護士ジェイクの苦悩を描く。子供を思う父親の気持ちを代弁するサミュエル・L・ジャクソンの熱演が胸を打つ。
6	ガンジー Gandhi 1982年　　インド	1980年、青年ガンジーはイギリス支配下の南アフリカの人種差別に怒りをおぼえ、抵抗運動を起こす。この運動を皮切りに、彼は人種差別撤廃の理想に燃え、インドでの反英不服従運動の指揮をとり、やがて英国の支配を終結させるのだが……。インド独立の偉大な指導者マハトマ・ガンジーの生涯を描いた伝記映画。
7	遠い夜明け Cry Freedom 1987年　イギリス	アパルトヘイト政策下の南アフリカを舞台に、ドナルド・ウッズが実体験に基づき描いた原作を映画化。黒人運動家のスティーブン・ピコを批判したことから、当人に会うことになった新聞社の編集長。ピコに会ったウッズは彼の人間性に惹かれ、アパルトヘイトへの現状が見えてくる。

異文化理解 おもしろクイズ 74　青い目茶色い目

Q. キング牧師が暗殺された1968年4月，小学3年生の担任ジェーン・エリオット先生は「黒人や先住民たちに対する強い差別意識を持ち続ける大人たちから子どもたちを守りたい」と考え，ある実験的な授業を試みました。これは子どもたちに差別される側の気持ちを実際に体験させるもので，子どもたちの人種差別に対する考えを大きく変えました。後に，この授業の様子を基にしたドキュメンタリーTV番組が制作され，*A Class Divided*（「青い目茶色い目」1985年，アメリカ）として放映されました．下の英文はこの授業の様子を表したものです。空所に適切な語を入れなさい。

　Jane Elliott started a special lesson just after Martin Luther King, Jr. was (　1　). She was a teacher of an elementary school, and she hoped that her students would come to find (　2　) terribly (　3　) and sad.

　First she (　4　) her students into two groups by the colors of their (　5　); blue or brown. Then she became prejudiced suddenly. She looked down on the children with brown eyes, while she praised the children with blue eyes.

　The boys and the girls, who had played together very happily, started to fight. Their (　6　) completely changed. Some felt low, looked sad and confused. The others looked like kings and queens. They made fun of their classmates with brown eyes.

　The next day Ms. Elliott changed her (　6　) toward the children. This time the children with brown eyes were kings and queens in her class.

　As a result, each child (　7　) the feeling of being discriminated against. This lesson by Ms. Elliott might be too tough for the children, but it was her strong will to stop discrimination that encouraged her to try it.

　The children were all white, and they were surely (　8　) by this lesson. Ms. Elliott continues to use this teaching method all over the country.

| ア．eyes | イ．killed | ウ．divided | エ．influenced |
| オ．wrong | カ．experienced | キ．attitude | ク．racism |

異文化理解 おもしろクイズ 75 Martin Luther King Quiz

Q. 以下のキング牧師についての簡単な紹介文を参考にして，それぞれの質問に答えなさい。ただし，4.は（　）に当てはまる適当な語句を選びなさい。

　1929年，米国南部のジョージア州アトランタに，バプテスト教会牧師の長男として生まれた。ボストン大学，ハーバード大学で神学と哲学を学んだ後，アラバマ州モントゴメリーの教会の牧師に就任。1955年，モントゴメリーで黒人女性ローザ・パークスが市条例違反で逮捕されたことに端を発する公民権運動の指導者として力を尽くす。ガンジーの哲学に共感し，キリスト教信仰に基づく独自の人種差別撤廃運動を推進。1963年の25万人の公民権運動支持者によるワシントン大行進を経て，1964年に公共施設や就職関係の差別撤廃をねらう「公民権法」が，1965年には選挙権行使上の差別をなくす「投票権法」が成立。1968年，遊説中に暗殺される。

1. How old was Martin Luther King when he led the boycott of segregated Montgomery buses?
   a. 26 years old　　　b. 36 years old　　　c. 46 years old

2. Where did Martin Luther King start his career?
   a. At a factory in Montgomery
   b. At a college in Montgomery
   c. At a church in Montgomery

3. Where did Martin Luther King give his famous 1963 "I Have a Dream" speech?
   a. During the March on Washington
   b. When he accepted the Nobel Peace Prize
   c. During the Montgomery Bus Boycott

4. Which word did Martin Luther King actually use in his 1963 speech? "I have a dream that one day this nation will rise up and live out the true meaning of its creed. We hold these truths to be self-evident: that all men are created (　　)."
   a. capable　　　b. equal　　　c. similar

5. What world-famous prize was Martin Luther King honored with?
   a. The Pulitzer Prize
   b. The Nobel Peace Prize
   c. The Nobel Prize for Chemistry

BOWWOW 一覧表

1	bowwow	dog	ワンワン
2	meow	cat	ニャーニャー
3	oink-oink	pig	ブーブー
4	moo	cow	モー
5	squeak	rat	チューチュー
6	cock-a-doodle-doo	rooster	コケコッコー
7	caw-caw	crow	カーカー
8	quack-quack	duck	ガーガー
9	chirp-chirp	sparrow	チュンチュン
10	croak croak	frog	ケロケロ
11	neigh	horse	ヒヒーン
12	baa baa	sheep	メェー
13	clap-clap	clap	パチパチ
14	brrr	tremble	ブルブル
15	Z-Z-Z	snore	グーグー
16	munch-munch	eat	ムシャムシャ
17	glug-glug	drink	ゴクゴク
18	ouch!	痛み	ウッ
19	oops!	しくじり	オット
20	gobble	がつがつ食べる	ガツガツ
21	achoo	sneeze	ハクション
22	boo hoo	子供が泣く	エーン
23	eek	叫び声	キャー
24	wow	歓喜	ワー
25	yahoo	歓声	ヤッター，ヤッホー
26	bla bla	早口	ペラペラ
27	kitchy-kitchy	くすぐり	コチョコチョ
28	cough cough	せき	コンコン
29	beep	車の警笛	ビー，プー
30	creak	きしむ音	キーキー
31	ting-a-ling-a-ling	bell	チリンチリン
32	ding-dong	bell	ピンポーン
33	tick-tock	clock	カチカチ
34	bang	door	バタン
35	splash	水のはねる音	パシャッ
36	thud	重いものが落ちる音	ドサッ，ズシン
37	twinkle	輝き	キラキラ
38	jingle-jingle	鈴やベルの音	ジャラジャラ
39	rum-pa-pum-pum	太鼓の音	トントン，ドンドン
40	smash	壊れる音	グシャッ

アメリカ人の知らない英語

		アメリカ人の知らない英語 (Japanese English)	American English	こんな勘違いが生じるかも…
1	食	カレーライス	curry and rice, curried rice	curryの語源はタミル語のkari「ソース，風味」
2		シュークリーム	cream puff	chou [仏] =「キャベツ」
3		ホットケーキ	pancake	
4		ソフトクリーム	soft ice cream	soft cream =「やわらかいクリーム」
5		アイスキャンディー	[米]popsicle　[英]ice lolly	
6		デコレーションケーキ	fancy cake	
7		サイダー(炭酸水)	soda, carbonated drink	cider =[米]りんごジュース，[英]りんご酒
8		ピーマン	green pepper, bell pepper	
9		フライドポテト	French fries	
10		モーニングサービス	breakfast special	morning service =「午前中の礼拝」
11		バイキング	buffet-style dinner	Viking =「海賊(8c～10c, ノルマン人)」 buffet [仏] =「細長いテーブル」
12	生活用品	電子レンジ	microwave oven	
13		ガスレンジ	gas-cooker	range =「範囲，向き」
14		クリーナー	vacuum cleaner	cleaner =「掃除作業員，洗浄剤」
15		ミキサー	blender	mixer =「音量調整係」
16		コンセント	(power) outlet	consent =「同意(する)」
17		ストーブ	heater	stove =「料理用レンジ」
18		ホットカーペット	electric carpet	
19		(スーパー)ファミコン	(Super) Nintendo	
20		リンス	conditioner	rinse =「すすぐ」
21		ナイトクリーム	skin care cream	
22		ヘルスメーター	(bathroom) scales	
23		アニメ	cartoon	animation =「活発，アニメ製作」
24		トランプ	cards	trump =「切り札」
25	学校	シール	sticker	seal =「印鑑，封印，密封」
26		ヒアリングテスト	listening comprehension test	hearing test =「聴力検査」
27		ペーパーテスト	written test, written exam	paper test =「紙質の検査」
28		マークシートテスト	computer-scored multiple-choice test	
29		カンニング	cheating, cribbing	cunning =「ずるい」
30		ボールペン	ball-point (pen)	
31		シャープペン	mechanical pencil	sharp pencil =「先の尖った鉛筆」
32		ホッチキス	stapler [英]	Hotchkiss =米国の発明者の名前
33		プリント	handout, printed material	
34		ノートパソコン	lap-top PC	
35		ネットショッピング	e-shopping	
36		ゼミ	seminar, lecture	
37		サークル	club	circle =「円」

		アメリカ人の知らない英語 (Japanese English)	American English	こんな勘違いが生じるかも…
38	住	マンション	apartment［米］, flat［英］	mansion =「大邸宅」
39		トイレ	bathroom	
40		ペンション	a small hotel	pension =「年金」
41	衣	トレーニングパンツ (トレパン)	sweat pants, gym slacks	training pants =「幼児の用便のしつけ用パンツ」
42		マフラー	scarf	muffler =「車の排気筒」
43		トレーナー	sweatshirt	trainer =「訓練する人，馬の調教師」
44		ワイシャツ	white shirt	
45		パンティーストッキング	panty hose, tights［英］	伝線する= ladder［米］, runner［英］
46		ノーアイロン	wash and wear	
47		ワンピース	dress	
48		ハイセンス	good taste	sense =「思慮分別，判断力」
49		ジャンパー	jacket	jumper =「ジャンプする人」
50	野球	ナイター	night game	
51		フォアボール	give a walk, walk	
52		キャッチボール	play catch	
53		チアガール	cheer leader	
55		デッドボール	hit by a pitch	
56	車	ガソリンスタンド	gas station	
57		ハンドル	steering wheel	handle =「カップなどの取っ手」
58		クラクション	horn	
59		サイドブレーキ	emergency brake	
60		ウィンカー	blinker, signals	
61		ライトバン	station wagon	
62		マイクロバス	minibus	
63		バックミラー	rearview mirror	
64	その他	ガードマン	(security) guard	
65		タレント	TV personality	talent =「才能(のある人)」
66		フリーター	part-time job	
67		アイドル	pop star	idol =「崇拝される人」
68		マニキュア(液)	nail polish	manicure =「爪や手の手入れをすること」
69		ナイーブ	sensitive	naïve =「世間知らずの，幼稚な」
70		ベテラン	expert	veteran =「退役軍人，老練な人」
71		プロポーション	nice body	proportion =「割合」
72		シルバーシート	seat for age	
73		ジェットコースター	roller coaster	
74		ファックス	fax, facsimileの短縮形	日本人の発音は性交［fuck(s)］に聞こえる
75		サラリーマン	office worker	
76		ボディチェック	security check	body check =レスリングなどで体当たりで相手の動きを止めること
78		フロント	reception	front =「建物の前」

		アメリカ人の知らない英語 (Japanese English)	American English	こんな勘違いが生じるかも…
79	その他	バーゲン	sales	bargain =「契約，取引，掘り出し物」
80		リサイクルショップ	secondhand store	
81		モーニングコール	wake-up call	
82		プラスアルファ	plus something, add something	
83		ゲームセンター	amusement arcade	
84		マスコミ	the mass media	
85		サラ金	loan shark	
86		イエスマン	apple polisher	
87		ヤンキー	punk	Yankee = アメリカ人の俗称
88		ブービー	the second last, next to the last	booby = マヌケ，とんま
89		キャスター（総合司会）	anchor person	
90		ビジネスホテル	economy hotel	
91		アトピー	dermatitis	
92		クリーニング	laundry	
93		フロンガス	chlorofluorocarbon	
94	英語以外の言語	オルゴール	music box	orgel［蘭］
95		ピンセット	tweezers	pincettes［仏］
96		ランドセル	little backpack	ransel［蘭］
97		スコップ	shovel	schop［蘭］
98		アンケート	questionnaire	enquete［仏］
100		ベランダ	balcony	veranda［ヒンズー語］
101		アベック	young couple	avec［仏］前置詞 = with
102		コンクール	contest, competition	concours［仏］「競争」
103		エチケット	good manner	etiquette［仏］
104		ピント	focus	punt［蘭］
105		ラジャー		了解（ラジャー）［中国の方言］
106		エステ	beauty clinic	esthe［仏］
107		カステラ	sponge cake	castilla［ポルトガル語］
108		アルバイト	part-time job	arbeit［独］「仕事，研究」
109		コロッケ	croquette	croquette［仏］
110		ピエロ	clown	pierrot［仏］
111		ノルマ	assignment（割り当て）	norma［露］
112		ピザパイ	pizza	pizza［伊］「パイ」= pie［英］「パイ」「パイパイ」と言っていることになる。

英語のことわざ

		上の句		下の句	日本語
1	☐☐☐☐	Seeing	☐☐☐☐	is believing.	百聞は一見にしかず
2	☐☐☐☐	Time	☐☐☐☐	is money.	時は金なり
3	☐☐☐☐	Love	☐☐☐☐	is blind.	あばたもえくぼ／恋は盲目
4	☐☐☐☐	No news	☐☐☐☐	is good news.	便りのないのはよい便り
5	☐☐☐☐	Health	☐☐☐☐	is better than wealth.	健康は富にまさる
6	☐☐☐☐	A friend in need	☐☐☐☐	is a friend indeed.	まさかの時の友が真の友
7	☐☐☐☐	Easy come,	☐☐☐☐	easy go.	悪銭身につかず
8	☐☐☐☐	First come,	☐☐☐☐	first served.	早い者勝ち
9	☐☐☐☐	Like father,	☐☐☐☐	like son.	かえるの子はかえる
10	☐☐☐☐	No pain,	☐☐☐☐	no gain.	まかぬ種は生えぬ
11	☐☐☐☐	Out of sight,	☐☐☐☐	out of mind.	去る者は日々に疎し
12	☐☐☐☐	So many men,	☐☐☐☐	so many minds.	十人十色
13	☐☐☐☐	When in Rome	☐☐☐☐	do as the Romans do.	郷に入りては郷に従え
14	☐☐☐☐	Slow and steady	☐☐☐☐	wins the race.	急がば回れ
15	☐☐☐☐	Strike	☐☐☐☐	while the iron is hot.	鉄は熱いうちに打て
16	☐☐☐☐	Kill two birds	☐☐☐☐	with one stone.	一石二鳥
17	☐☐☐☐	When the cat's away	☐☐☐☐	the mice will play.	鬼のいぬ間の洗濯
18	☐☐☐☐	There is no smoke	☐☐☐☐	without fire.	火のないところに煙は立たず
19	☐☐☐☐	The pen is mightier	☐☐☐☐	than the sword.	ペンは剣よりも強し
20	☐☐☐☐	All work and no play	☐☐☐☐	makes Jack a dull boy.	よく遊び，よく学べ
21	☐☐☐☐	Hunger	☐☐☐☐	is the best sauce.	空腹にまずいものなし
22	☐☐☐☐	It is no use	☐☐☐☐	crying over spilt milk.	覆水盆に返らず
23	☐☐☐☐	Bad news	☐☐☐☐	travels fast.	悪事千里を走る
24	☐☐☐☐	A drowning man	☐☐☐☐	will catch at a straw.	おぼれる者は藁をもつかむ

	上の句	下の句	日本語
25	☐☐☐☐ All is well	☐☐☐☐ that ends well.	終わりよければすべてよし
26	☐☐☐☐ Birds of a feather	☐☐☐☐ flock together.	類は友を呼ぶ
27	☐☐☐☐ The early bird	☐☐☐☐ catches the worm.	早起きは三文の得
28	☐☐☐☐ Make hay	☐☐☐☐ while the sun shines.	日の照るうちに干草を作れ
29	☐☐☐☐ Necessity	☐☐☐☐ is the mother of invention.	必要は発明の母
30	☐☐☐☐ A rolling stone	☐☐☐☐ gathers no moss.	転石苔むさず
31	☐☐☐☐ Speech is silver,	☐☐☐☐ silence is gold.	雄弁は銀，沈黙は金
32	☐☐☐☐ A stitch in time	☐☐☐☐ saves nine.	転ばぬ先の杖
33	☐☐☐☐ Too many cooks	☐☐☐☐ spoil the broth.	船頭多くして船山に登る
34	☐☐☐☐ Where there is a will,	☐☐☐☐ there is a way.	精神一到何事かならざらん
35	☐☐☐☐ A sound mind	☐☐☐☐ in a sound body.	健全なる精神は健全なる肉体に宿る
36	☐☐☐☐ An apple a day	☐☐☐☐ keeps the doctor away.	リンゴ一個で医者知らず
37	☐☐☐☐ Walls	☐☐☐☐ have ears.	壁に耳あり障子に目あり
38	☐☐☐☐ Time	☐☐☐☐ flies like an arrow.	光陰矢のごとし
39	☐☐☐☐ Look	☐☐☐☐ before you leap.	石橋を叩いて渡る
40	☐☐☐☐ Honesty	☐☐☐☐ in the best policy.	正直が最良の策
41	☐☐☐☐ Don't count your chickens	☐☐☐☐ before they are hatched.	とらぬ狸の皮算用
42	☐☐☐☐ Practice	☐☐☐☐ makes perfect.	習うより慣れよ
43	☐☐☐☐ Every rule	☐☐☐☐ has some exceptions.	例外のない規則はない
44	☐☐☐☐ Custom	☐☐☐☐ is second nature.	習慣は第二の天性
45	☐☐☐☐ Knowledge	☐☐☐☐ is power.	知は力なり
46	☐☐☐☐ Rome was not built	☐☐☐☐ in a day.	ローマは一日にしてならず
47	☐☐☐☐ Spare the rod	☐☐☐☐ and spoil the child.	かわいい子には旅をさせよ
48	☐☐☐☐ Heaven helps	☐☐☐☐ those who help themselves.	天は自らを助くる者を助く

異文化理解
おもしろクイズ

ISBN978-4-7589-2306-4　C7082

著作者	永 倉 由 里	［英文校閲：David W. Hunt, Jennifer Hansen］
発行者	武 村 哲 司	
印刷所	日之出印刷株式会社	

2004年5月20日　第1版第1刷発行©
2018年3月10日　第2版第4刷発行

発行所　株式会社 開拓社　〒113-0023　東京都文京区向丘1-5-2
電話　(03) 5842-8900　(代表)
振替　00160-8-39587
http://www.kaitakusha.co.jp